Reading the Flowers

OTHER BOOKS BY LINDA FRANCE

POETRY COLLECTIONS
Red (Bloodaxe, 1992)
The Gentleness of the Very Tall (Bloodaxe, 1994)
Storyville (Bloodaxe, 1997)
The Simultaneous Dress (Bloodaxe, 2002)
The Toast of the Kit-Cat Club (Bloodaxe, 2005)
book of days (Smokestack, 2009)
You are Her (Arc Publications, 2010)

PAMPHLETS
Aerogramme (Talking Pen, 2004)
wild (Sand Press, 2004)
The Moon & Flowers (Queens Hall Arts Centre, 2008)
Through the Garden Gate (NCLA, 2011)
Border Song (Hareshaw Press, 2012)
another wild (Hareshaw Press, 2014)

ANTHOLOGIES
(AS EDITOR)
Sixty Women Poets (Bloodaxe, 1993)
Sauce (The Poetry Virgins, Bloodaxe, 1994)
Rowing Home (Cruse Bereavement Care, 2008)

LINDA FRANCE
Reading the Flowers

2016

Published by Arc Publications,
Nanholme Mill, Shaw Wood Road
Todmorden OL14 6DA, UK
www.arcpublications.co.uk

Design by Tony Ward
Printed in Great Britain by
TJ International, Padstow, Cornwall

978 1910345 49 8 (pbk)
978 1910345 50 4 (hbk)
978 1910345 51 1 (ebook)

Cover photograph by Karen Melvin

Editor for the UK and Ireland:
John W. Clarke

ACKNOWLEDGEMENTS

Reading the Flowers draws on several years of botanical wanderings, for which I am grateful to Arts Council England, Cove Park, the Institute of Advanced Study at Durham University and Durham Book Festival, Newcastle University, New Writing North and the Leverhulme Trust.

Thanks to Ajahns Abhinando and Sucitto, Moniza Alvi, Colette Bryce, Vicki Feaver, Linda Thake and the Women Poets Group in Newcastle for being my first readers. Also to gardening friends, Sue Dunne, Anabel Gammidge, Rosie Hudson, Karen Melvin and Susie White, Corbridge Gardening Society, Dilston Physic Garden and everyone at Moorbank for their expertise and encouragement.

I am particularly appreciative of hospitality shown me at Botanic Gardens in Padua, Singapore, Sydney, Tokyo (Shinjuku Gyoen), Pisa, Oxford, Kew, Durham, Edinburgh, Benmore, Dawyck, Logan, Glasgow and Linn.

Thanks to Alec Peever for 'A Story You Tell After Dinner' and his sculpture inscribed with a variation on 'In the Arid House' (haunted here by Shelley's 'Ozymandias'). A phrase from Robert Frost's 'The Death of The Hired Man' is grafted into the end of 'Haw Medicine'. 'Puzzle' celebrates the Reverend John Galbraith Graham (1921-2013), crossword compiler, better known as Araucaria (better known as the monkey puzzle tree).

Versions of some of these poems have previously appeared in *another wild, Black Light Engine Room, Culture / The Journal, dhamma moon, Earthwords* (Friends of the Earth), *Gift* (A Chapbook for Seamus Heaney), *The Guardian, Mslexia, The North, Plumwood Mountain Journal, poeticabotanica* (blog), *Poetics of the Archive* (NCLA), *Poetry International, Poetry Review, Screaming Steel (Art, War and Trauma), Shadowscript, Through the Garden Gate, Urthona, You are Her* (Arc Publications) and *Lindisfarne: Poetry in Progress* on BBC Radio 4.

'Bernard and Cerinthe', 'Husbandry and 'Stone Meadow' won First Prizes in the National Poetry Competition 2013, Larkin and East Riding Poetry Prize 2012, and the Yorkshire Open 2012 respectively.

People from a planet without flowers would think we must be mad with joy the whole time to have such things about us.

Iris Murdoch

CONTENTS

CUT FLOWERS

If I raid my stash of seed catalogues,
      flower books – wild and tamed, glossy hybrids –
            to spend the night with a blade, cutting
out marigolds, lupins, sweet peas, snapdragons
      till the floor's littered with stems and petals,
            snippings and spaces where flowers once bloomed,
a life's work couldn't make enough beds
      or bouquets to lay bare the garden inside me
            I invite you now to enter.
Step across the carpet of petunias and fuchsias,
      flowers that blush on our behalf –
            see how they all cleave to you,
charge your heart – this, my highest currency.

EUCALYPTUS

Eucalyptus niphophila

Standing beside the tallest tree in the garden
you grow smaller. It's as big
as the place it started from;
the whole antipodes mapped
on its moulting trunk.
It's grown out of its skin.
You lean back to watch the leaves,
ticklish against the sky, shivering,
it's so high and far from home.

The doctor comes with his stethoscope.
My mother comes with the Vicks.
She rubs some on my chest, pyjama jacket up,
winceyette lifted clear of the sticky stuff,
her strong hands, her wedding ring.
My eyes water.
The room smells of trees.

I bow forward to let her reach my back.
In the bedroom cold enough I can pluck
the feathers of every breath, my body
warms and I want her
never to stop as I melt with the balm
of how close she is,
how it almost hurts.

You stoop to gather the fallen cups
of seeds, clustered on dry stalks,
you'll set in a blue glass jar.
Call it a spell

against sleeplessness,
the bruise of white rabbit dreams
chased down a hole
spiralling deep underground
to the other side of your world.

LILY

Named after a flower, you were a gardener
without a garden. You filled our flat –
proudly called a *maisonette* – with flora,
histories of courage and abundance.

The windowsill was home for a mother
of thousands, a gift from your friend, Phyllis,
Pearl's money tree, some Tradescantia.

Dad grew taller, praising your green fingers.
I'd inspect your hands – the only evidence,
those plants you'd tend and tether like children.

Now when I look, my own open palms
are turning into yours, empty and worn
but for the blessings of friends, this emerald planet,
the unfathomable mulch of compost.

ANTHOLOGY

I never met my great-grandmother
Mary, who couldn't write her name –
    nothing but a shy, shaky cross
    on the creased marriage certificate;

only knew my grandmother Dora
from scratched sepia – her young face
    telling her story better than any
    document, a family's secrets.

Self-heal, speedwell, meadowsweet,
lady's mantle and *heartsease* –
    I'm gathering what I can for them,
    recording their names in print:

fragile charms of petal and ink
to braid those lines lost between us
back into wild, breathing life.

    This life, the only flower I have.

FLORESCENCE

If time is measured in poured light,
this summer's splashing through my hands
faster than I can weed. Or write

the names of the plants in bloom –
Daisy, Iris, Rose – like friends
in an old photograph, one June,

taking a walk round the garden,
sharing a secret, heads leant
together. Posies, white ribbon.

Any of our grandmothers,
they're washed away in a torrent,
this unseasonable weather

that seeds the air with a fresh smell,
the slow stretch of girls who'll wander
here when I've gone home to the soil,

girls with names grown under glass –
Fern, Strelitzia, Oleander;
tomorrow's light, petals on the grass.

ATLAS CEDAR

Cedrus atlantica

A long way from the mountains,
possible return routes
signposted all over me, home

is a corner where blue isn't
blue, and green
isn't green, my arms

a tangle
of glaucous stars,
cones like planets orbiting.

I keep my scent
locked in my trunk,
balsamic,

prayerful.
You'd think the crazy barking
of the dogs next door

might spark homesickness.
On the contrary,
they comfort me.

I catch the longing in their throats,
let it dapple my limbs
like itinerant sunlight.

NEST

Tattered by wear, age and weather,
this wasp-wrought monument
is a confection of layers – each swathe
of fibre striated, like chocolate rippled
through cream; each distinct arc
an accretion of light and shade.
Wood regurgitated delivers
a new substance to the world.

And so much world in it:
wave upon wave engraved by Hokusai;
dried fungi on a market stall in Italy;
woodshavings from a Scottish workshop;
the seamed felt of a jacket built to withstand
the snows of Mongolia; wind's rhythm
through caves in Cappadocia;
Silk Route's *Diamond Sutra*,
the oldest book in history.

On paper, it's easy to summon places
we might take shelter, settle –
as if the wasps (those clever ten thousand
wasps) have penned a libretto
of our horizons, this earth's encyclopedia.

Too large to hold aloft in one hand,
like Hamlet, and interrogate,
the intimations of skull, of bone,
are undeniable. Stray waspish corpses
adhere to crevice, cobweb, feather.

I lift it between shelf and table, precious
as a newborn; look through the botanical
lens and let my eyes be widened
by the theatrical and factual,
till I want to fly on veined and layered wings
right to the heart of it, and plant myself
like a seed in the loam of its mind.

SCRIBBLY GUM

Eucalyptus haemastoma

Scribbly Gum Moths
tuck their eggs between layers
of bark, old and new. Larvae
wriggle out, burrow into
the trunk's fresh skin for food,
tunnels growing as they do.
Travelling back, the same route,
their trail stops when they turn into
wing factory, chrysalis.
Old bark shed, what's left
are their rusty tracks, particular
as fingerprints, charts
to monitor a restless heart.

It's a struggle to write *past, address,*
next: none of them match
this tree's palimpsest of flight,
its brave and senseless rhythms;
nor map the way I'm burrowing
into gaps between old
and new. How many lifetimes
to decipher my own
scribbling, fathom those spaces
where a plane took off,
that bud opened, the end
of this blood-smudged
zig-zag line?

ADAPTATION

Some days it's all wanting, wanting
        what you haven't got, this rainforest summer,
dense with the diminishing currency
        of clouds. Caught between resistance
and surrender, the more that you want
        is a walk in the jungle, where you peel off
your city clothes and lean into wet fronds
        till you reach the red stem you barely know
the name of, stroke the waxy lacquer
        of its bracts, like no petals you've ever seen,
and feel its power claw through you.
        Like a hermit hummingbird, you drink
the liquor in its chevron of scarlet cups,
        tassels of flowers brushing your lips,
each tipped with an eye dark enough
        to pin you to the centre of where you are
in the world's spinning marketplace.
        If you can stomach its Amazonian medicine,
it'll ferry you to the edge of words, let you be
        friends with the earth's tilt – not getting what
you think you want, blossoming beyond
        small ideas about growth, slaking your thirst
on looking – and find some rest there.

TALKING ABOUT THE WEATHER

The gardener sat on the old wicker chair,
hands wrapped round a mug of nettle tea –

and even though the room was warm, curtains
drawn against the night, the way we hold
our breath between winter and what might follow –

snowmelt, rainfall, lambing storm, the words
she spoke flung open the door on water, a river
in spate, rushing and roaring between us –

her worst fears of flood and disaster,
an unstoppable lostness sweeping her away,
tossed in the current of truth, lies, testing

the strength of this earth we cling to – as if our lives
were leaves, whispering *North, North, North.*

THE STRAWBERRY TREE

Arbutus unedo

On Bosch's paradise tree carmine berries
wink on dark stems beside waxy bells,
a tumble of cream and pink. Its name
admits the fruit tastes of nothing –
one berry enough, food fit for birds.

At the end of November snow fell,
snow like no one had seen before;
an Eden lost while the sky slept.

The old tree couldn't bear the weight
of its white coverlet, creaking till its trunk
and branches split, exposed the chilled bones
of a dying year.
     Earth scarred
under their boots, the gardeners went back
to work, tramping through snow with sawn
and fallen boughs to coax into smoke.

Flames shone on their faces as the fire took hold;
flakes of ash fingered their shoulders like frost.
The incense of burnt heartwood rose.
As if such wild heat could melt a hole
in the heavens, another night was lost to snow.

Sturdy souls till the calendar with spades
and hoes, tell the legend of that winter,
the snow, the fire, the strawberry tree.

THE OLDEST GARDEN IN THE WORLD

Orto Botanico di Padova

Hortus conclusus, Our Mother's garden:
a roof of blue silk, medicine for the eyes;

her photosynthesis – given and giving back.
The space between your arms conceives

a circle. St. Anthony and Justina call
to each other across spires of magnolia,

the tired fountains, minutiae of gravel.
Time slips away and we shuck off

our unnecessary selves, let them hang
draped on the railings while we dance

like these fruits of the hovenia, more
or less human; our partners – Japanese

anemones, *Ruby Moon*, the hyacinth bean.
After rain, the tang of tamped dust, and

your heart translates into *foglia*, opening.
Five hundred years old, still unfinished.

HELICONIA

Here is your ticket to the cloud forest,
        where trees speak parrot and liana; an insect

that sounds like a vehicle reversing
        will keep you alert to the sheen of creepers

and the smell of earth, liquorice, after rain.
        Walk in the tracks of a man who loved

bananas and tied his shoes with blue irises.
        Here nothing you do will be under glass.

You can choose your own mother. Sisters too
        are in accordance with preference. You will

have nine. This is a mountain of your own
        mind, history and geography rephotographed –

see! – you will be sporting a pith helmet
        to clarify your dependence on oxygen. Soon

a beam beyond the UV spectrum will radiate
        from your thoracic cavity, attracting sunbirds

and butterflies from an extensive radius. They will rest
        on your extremities, the crown of your hat

in particular. Observed from a distance,
        like synchronized swimmers, they will spell

the word for this darkness, where garden begins.

§

The words they use: *perpetual summer,*
endless growth, guaranteed survival –
as soon as there's too much of anything,
your mind snaps shut, nothing stays natural.

Endless growth, guaranteed survival –
among so many flowers, loneliness:
your mind snaps shut. Is nothing natural?
Copper light in the star-apple trees.

Among so many flowers, loneliness;
some bloom for only a single day.
Copper light in the star-apple trees,
torch ginger setting fire to green.

Some bloom only for a single day,
ribbed and veined like our own bodies.
Torch ginger sets fire to green.
Palms are fans, windmills, feathers.

Ribbed and veined like our own bodies,
all the trees are multi-tasking.
Are palms fans? Windmills? Feathers?
There's garden and there's its opposite.

All the trees are multi-tasking –
labels rehearse their use. *Perpetual summer.*
There's garden and there's its opposite
as soon as there's too much of anything.

§

When the sun's at its peak, what we need
is shade. It makes squirrels of us all.
We are animal and contingent,
nosing down unfamiliar smells.

Shade makes squirrels of us all.
Tree roots are wily as crocodiles.
We nose down unfamiliar smells,
past palms with elephants' feet and ears.

With tree roots wily as crocodiles,
this heat's conducive to great stillness.
Up in palms with elephant feet, hear
insects beep like life-support machines.

In the heat, conducive to great stillness,
butterflies pretend to be petals,
the insect life-support machine beeps
while a beetle dribbles nectar.

Butterflies pretend to be petals.
The drongo displays his long black tail.
A dark blue beetle dribbles white nectar.
The turtles are always hungry.

A drongo displays his long black tail.
When the sun peaks, what is it we need?
The turtles are always hungry.
I too am animal, contingent.

§

You can't hear what you've left behind
above the racket of birds, insects
and the endless static beyond
what you remember as silence.

Above the racket of birds, insects
illuminate the night garden.
All you remember is silence,
monochrome, a dream's frequency.

Illuminated, the night garden
revolves around a banyan tree,
monochrome. Don't dreams frequently
replay old dramas of lostness?

Revolving round the banyan tree,
you negotiate arrival,
rewinding old dramas of lostness,
anchored by twisted aerial roots.

Once negotiated, arrival
fast-forwards into departure,
anchored only by aerial roots
or, on the wing, bats' sonar instinct.

Fast-forward into *Departures*.
You can't hear what you're leaving behind:
on the wing, a bat's sonar instinct;
endless static beyond listening.

HANAMI

Woken by rain
my first thought
cherry blossom!

>   *each meeting
>   a single chance*

The umbrellas
of Tokyo –
precision choreography

>   the most photographed trees
>   in the world

A bottle
of hot green tea
soothing my hands

>   still in full bloom
>   branches' shadows

Turtles bask
on the margins
of stone and water

>   out of nowhere
>   a white egret

Two bridges
and the path between –
where we live

>   tannoys play their last tune
>   *Auld Lang Syne!*

SETTLER

This landscape is full of crossroads. You lie
flat on your back at one of them, letting
gravity mould your trunk's length to the curve
of the earth's shoulder. If trees are signposts,
these point to Chile, the deserts of Arizona,
Taiwan; far east spun round to near north.
A foghorn sounds down in the Harbour.

Low to the ground, where even the grass
has a foreign habit, you could allow yourself
to be soothed by the smell of cypress, hearty
and resinous; maybe pick up a handful of cones,
all fibre and sinew, as if carved from what's masked
by human skin. In the pocket of your rucksack
they might act as a talisman of arrival, landing;

of not knowing where, just now, in this place
of sap, persistent insects and raucous birds,
sub-tropical heat strong enough to release
a tree from history and set its fragrance free.
Unaccountable. Rest now, sleep beneath it,
settled in the open house of its many stems,
the shady compass of roots and leaves.

SPOTTED GUM CAMOUFLAGE

Corymbia maculata

On a city street you practise the art
of visual deception, trying to match
peeling walls, splotched gutters. The urban world
has taken you as one of its lost tribe
but you can't disguise how much longer, deeper
you've known this land than the human creatures
who scratch their names on your trunk, shadows
of their own scars.
                    You outspan them,
strafing the rooftops; your skin
a map of Australia, New Holland,
Gondwana, this earth – as many wounds
as words.
            You, who can ration water, survive
the invasion of sunlight, live on
safer ground in the bush where fire can lift
the lid off your cups of seeds. Here you will
divulge smudges of gum, secret patches
of blue in your bark archipelagos;
pieces of a puzzle scattered to crack
the perfect answer; your jacket less flak-flak
than mottled suede, peace-loving, abstract.

Today we have naming of plants. Yesterday
we had raising the flag. And tomorrow morning
we shall have what to do with the prisoners. But today,
today we have naming of plants. Lilly-pilly
sets pink saucers of sweetness all around Botany Bay.
      And thus we revive the glory of jam.

These are *Grevillea, Hakea*. And these,
Brunonia, Blandfordia, whose use you will see
when the Endeavour commands. And these are *Calandrinia*,
which the natives call para-keel-ya. Bu-jor
is Melaleuca the people here use for mattresses
      and dressing wounds, swaddling newborns.

This is *Hibbertia*, named after George Hibbert,
London merchant, one of our most generous patrons.
I don't want to hear anyone call it its common name –
    Climbing
Guinea Flower. This is our land, paid for with our coin.
Most of the blackfellas die of smallpox. Some just disappear.
      Those that survive learn the King's English.

And this little beauty is *Darwinia*. I don't need
to tell you who it celebrates. No, not that one –
his grandfather. Isn't botany a system based on class,
the natural order of dynasty and empire?
We will remove the Cabbage Tree Palms and lose the emu,
ship the rebels' heads back home.

Back to Sir Joseph Banks, the reason we're here today,
naming the plants, in our own image – Old Man Banksia,
Swamp Banksia, Acorn Banksia, Cut Leaf Banksia –
stubborn, ambitious. Note their spikes and cones, exotic
    blooms
in his *Florilegium* – wiri-ya-gan, wad-ang-gari.
For today we have the naming of plants.

Tot it up:
1 Transit of Venus
370 tonnes of Endeavour
94 souls – one captain, two lieutenants,
      master and boatswain (their two mates),
      surgeon and carpenter (one mate each),
      gunner, cook, clerk, steward,
      two quarter-masters, armourer, sailmaker,
      three midshipmen, forty-one able seamen,
      twelve marines and nine servants
One astronomer
Two naturalists, three artists and four field assistants
(38 men who'd never see home again)
Two dogs, a sackful of chickens and one already much-trav-
    elled goat
Five more artists back in England, plus eighteen engravers
£7000 from Joseph Banks' own purse
1974 First draft in black and white
1988 Final draft, full colour, *à la poupée*
2 months per plate (738)
200 years late

                         (fanfare of trumpets)
        Banks' Florilegium: A Publication
        In Thirty-Four Parts
        Copper Plate Engravings of Plants
        Collected On Captain Cook's First Voyage
        Round the World

No wonder, when Miguel unlocks the door
to the Special Collection and locates
the buckram bound folio containing Plate 276
and there it is in front of me – *Botany Bay,*
Australia, 29 April – 6 May 1770,
Lambertia formosa – the fringed pink cup
of the Mountain Devil that only a week before,
hiking in the Blue Mountains, Donna told me
was bush tucker and showed me how
to suck out its fresh nectar,

for a second time I feel my senses erupt, shift
into a new landscape, glacial, tectonic.
Dumbstruck, I drink it in, counting every cent.

ANT LANGUAGE

Lord knows it's easy to fall in love
with cicadas and katydids, day and night
tuning me in to the Southern Cross,
soundtrack for *Englishwoman Abroad*.
Pollen-collecting clouds of native bees,
stingless, also sweeten my squeamish heart.

Tougher summoning kindness for the ants,
a segmented phalanx queuing up on
the kitchen windowsill to come forage
for whatever looks tasty to an ant –
a whisker of catfood smiling on a spoon,
the tiniest lick of apricot jam;

a crust of raisin bread, agreed HQ.
Or outdoors, crawling between my toes,
up my arms – an unacceptable degree
of wriggle – to bite down, unprovoked,
on tender flesh with practised mandibles.
The way they file so industriously

one behind the other offends my view
of things – anthropocentric, programmed
to Individual Freedom. I could
maybe learn some ant manners, division
of labour, cooperative spirit.
But my stung right wrist has swelled

to the size of an antique library and
their creeping looks too much like words
appearing on a screen of their own accord,
words I can't read, inverted, experimental.
I could be more curious, attend more
closely, study ant grammar, the conditional.

It's a long path, aspiring to love the ant,
sugar ant, bull ant, even the yellow crazy ant.
Gentler to tread if I remember how they help
half the plants here in Australia spread:
the way a shift will drag a seed
to their underground nest, feed their young

and devour what flesh is left; leave the germ
to settle, in its own time, take root,
long after the ant employed in such labour
has ascended to wherever ants gather
to lie down and rest. And that's, let's face it,
before I even consider the cockroach,

its unforgivable nocturnal slang.

TENDRIL

As if someone who isn't me is tuning
a radio, I hear a checkout girl
        aisles away call a customer *Flower* –

the vowels innocent, as if a child
had said it, and kind, plucked from the air
        Just for You, a tender Geordie dipthong;

one of those words Dad would let fly
from his mouth like magic and watch me
        sprout a crown of petals. Here, in Morrisons

on the Shields Road, I hear it echo, *Flower*
Flower Flower, swelling onto the shelves
        of bleach and polish, the rows and rows

and rows of beans, into the bakery and
where they keep the cheese, over the fruit
        and veg and the fish, slack-lipped. Its pale

and lovely fragrance languishes around
the newspaper stand and the lottery till,
        licks its way out the door into the car park,

petrol station, cash machine, up the street,
over the roundabout and along the Wall,
        until all the back end of Byker's a garden

but, however hard I try, I can't pick up
the channel – the actual burr and timbre
        of my father's voice, what he sounded like.

SELF-PORTRAIT AS A CASE OF STICK INSECTS

Phasmatodea

As long as I stay invisible, I am everything
you don't know. A casual glance won't unpick

my lock – this glass case of bramble stalks,
prickly, soaked. I'm an illusionist, arrow

and cross-bow, plant or insect, a specialist
at playing dead. Woody in winter, independent,

I strew my fatherless eggs disguised as seeds
on the leaves beneath me. All my girls

are silk, small preparatory sketches. Blind
to night and day, they twitch and skitter

slowly, practise disappearing. I've lost
a leg, as if I were growing into my own

brittle pretence. The longer you look,
the more you'll see – this whole case transparent,

crawling with what you're certain can't be phantoms.

IN THE ARID HOUSE

The desert codex is best read at night –
by starlight you see more and farther,
follow your heart's compass, what might
be shed, as you dream your way home – Atacama,
Kalahari, Sahara, white
sand, yellow stone, constellations
of cacti and succulents, bobcat
and coyote – our ancestral navigations.

Listen. Your body's every cell
senses darkness opening the pores scattered
on leaf and stem, hears the suck of breath. Feel
the spectre of water etch your face, play
out the breath of your days – that vast galaxy.
The lone and level sands stretch far away.

BERNARD AND CERINTHE

If a flower is always a velvet curtain
onto some peepshow he never opens,

it's a shock to find himself, sheltering
from the storm in a greenhouse,

seduced by a leaf blushing blue
at the tips, begging to be stroked.

He's caught in the unfamiliar ruffle
of knickerbockers or petticoat, a scent

of terror, vanilla musk. If he were
not himself, he'd let his trembling lips

articulate the malleability of wax;
the bruise of bracts, petals, purple

shrimps; seeds plump as buttocks,
tucked out of harm's way, cocos-de-mer

washed up off Curieuse or Silhouette.
But being Bernard, he's dumbstruck,

a buffoon in front of a saloon honey
high-kicking the can-can. Can't-can't.

He attempts to cool himself, thinking
about seahorses, *Hippocampus erectus*,

listening to the rain refusing to stop,
soft against the steamed-up glass.

FLOWER PRESS

It pricked her from the inside,
the bud she'd been taught
was white and perfect.

In the end she gave it away, casually,
the only thing that was hers,
as if it were nothing,
a paperback she'd finished reading
and didn't want to keep.

She didn't know if it were leaves
or petals asking to be freed
that left the stain,
a pressed flower.

Nothing about the curtained room
was familiar – not even the boy
who pruned so assiduously.

The diary she drew a cartoon daisy in
was also lost, stolen or surrendered,
gone up in flames.

MEADOW FRITILLARY

Fritillaria Meleagris

An upside down loving cup,
        you're a perfect suck for a bumble bee

or this finger I slip in and stir you with.
        Some call you *Chequered*

Daffodil. You blush, the latticework
on your cheeks pixilated, a cross-pollination

of fritter and frill. Not at all like a *Snake's Head*.
Throat dry with admiring, I try a whisper –

*Chess Flower, Frog-cup, Leper Lily,
Guinea Hen*. No answer. Petalled oracle,

box of dice, I want you to tell my fortune,
bring me luck, this sun forever on my back

and nothing but you to think about;
like kisses, all your wondrous names.

HUSBANDRY

Even though we're both wives, married
to each other, we follow a recipe,
three thousand years old. A taste of the past,
my dearest says, and also what's ahead.

As summer's losing her thread, we trawl
the hedgerows for brambles, sloes, hips
and haws, our fingers pricked with picking.
We lick away each other's stains.

Our zinc bucket's nearly full; the rim,
a silver *O* of hope, a wedding ring.

According to Democritus, we must preserve
the seeds in honey – an amber hive
of eggs – and lower in a length of rope,
let it soak while we work up a sweat,

digging a trench to bury our twist
of sweetness where we'll be enclosed.
X marks the spot, the stretch of lawn
where we like to sit, watch the sun set.

Behind us there'll be thorns, an edge
to hold two souls, our honey hedge.

HEDGEROW JELLY

The morning seemed ordinary
until she lifted the sieve of fruit – each berry
plucked from the hedgerows, 'goodly
amounts' of hawthorn and rosehip, according to the recipe
necessary
for pectin to set the jelly,
tumbled with apples from the city –
and dripping through the muslin was ruby,
pure and concentrated autumn, fiery,
bloody,
waiting for sugar and another boiling, bubbly
and foaming, till she wanted to dive into the beautifully
maroon confection bursting into life in the shiny
saucepan, her whole kitchen rich and smelly
with harvest bounty
she skimmed and poured into jars, steamy
with anticipation, fumes rising billowy
and sweet, like the spills, sticky,
she licked from her fingers before holding her trophy –
three glinting garnet jars, lovely –
up to the light, too rosy
to seal in with a label saying its name so plainly

WOOD-BATHING

Even late in the year you grasp the gift
of it – cortisol, blood sugar, pulse

settling as you walk and breathe in
whatever the trees breathe out

on a day bright as washed glass;
the glancing spangles on a brazen

sweetgum, handspan leaves trembling.
Whiskers of pine glitter against

your irises; a birch's ginger you want
to photograph and keep, you

who can't keep track of your own breath,
shallow and ragged, with a mind of its own.

Let this be enough, this organic exchange
of oxygen and subtle odours

no one can quantify. The Japanese
call it 'wood-bathing', *shinrin-yoku*,

as if it were an art or a medicine.
Take daily – forest, arbour, garden, park.

BLACK CATKINS

Salix gracilistyla melanostachys

I give the student collecting
for the Red Cross in Japan
a scatter of change from my purse.

The young man bows and hands me
an origami crane – orange folds
the colour of today's flames

as we burn the spring clearing
on the other side of the hollow
where the black catkins grow.

The sun has real heat in it
we're grateful for – and the birds
are trilling, honey bees grazing.

The willow risks new leaves;
its catkins' black, broken by pollen
exploding, pale dust settling.

News from Fukushima follows me
here – the emergency increased
to 5 to allow for *wider implications;*

not just our gardens, this whole earth
a vast and shallow bowl we think
is ours to fill with implications

we're surprised to see spilling over.

A STORY YOU TELL AFTER DINNER

Oxford Botanic Garden, September 2001

It happens when you're up a ladder,
jewelling letters chiselled into stone,
ten storeys above this city you love,
Magdalen Bridge flowing over the Cherwell.
Precarious has *precious* hidden inside it.
You keep your balance, at risk of losing
those wisps of gold leaf, too thin for fingers,
wind's greedy breath. Maybe it's just then,
working on the circle of an *a*, crease
of an *r*, when the builder starts with
his effing and blinding – a rant you've heard
before: till someone else calls you down
and repeats it all in different words.

You pack up early, sit in the pick-up,
fiddle with the radio. Driving back is out
of the question. You walk under the arch
into the garden, aiming for its still
bubbling heart, the fall of water, as if that
might wash away the stain of smoke
and rumour. The leaves are just
beginning to catch fire, so much tinder
in the blue of the sky. Staying alive
might be enough – breathing oxygen
and slow centuries of balance, skill,
brick upon brick of faith in the future.
Till you can trust your legs, arms, eyes

to take you home to gather up your precious ones.

WHAT THE TREES REMEMBER

We were roar then
spark and shrapnel

lost to birdsong
nails hammered in

We were for more
than this

charcoal and ash
felled and fallen

Paper a traitor
to our names

history refusing
to be noted

We remembered
we had roots

and they called us
back into leaf

ITALIAN ANCESTRY

The oldest magnolia in Europe
dissolves the last of the light
from the west. True to its name,
sempreverde, all its strength rests

in the surface of its polished leaves.
Dusty cones plained and purled
by grandmothers in coral and citrus
will see it through the winter.

The whole tree is a domed basilica,
sun filtering through stained glass
foliage, drawing my eyes up
to the heavens it knows is home.

Sit here long enough, I'll hear it talk
in tongues. Until then, let the bark
be a frieze of fallen angels; safe in a notch,
a sacred heart. Roots fall away

from the sturdy trunk like lost souls
I can follow back to their source.
I know this because here I am
one of them, found, evergreen.

WHITE POPLAR IN GOLD LIGHT

Populus alba

All day I carry it round in my head,
a halo of precious and priceless,
regretting my mind is autumn, must
shed even these astonishments.

I want to slip it on my finger – *there* –
ductile, platinum, twenty-four carat,
where I can thread myself through its lightness
and (flesh and bone) bear the weight of it.

SWEET GUM

Liquidambar styraciflua

It takes the louche cool
of late summer on the heel
of a long-drawn-out
drought to bring out the best
in a leaf
before it sets free its ghost.

When desire isn't all
that matters, then fall
is the deciduous rise
to the surface
of carotene, anthocyanin
or xanthophyll,

silenced till now by the clamour
of chlorophyll. And even this
sweetness must be lost –
a red lament of abandon,
defiance,
indeed, utterly natural.

MAIDENHAIR

Ginkgo biloba

Under the year's first snow
the garden's in hiding.

Its white silhouette
confounds the eye

aching for delight, clarity,
a dark glass it can see

its own fullness in.
The yellow confetti

of ginkgo leaves,
a gesture towards

definition, is oblique
as a Chinese oracle:

a flock of ochre moths
drawn to pinpricks

of frozen light;
notched wings, half-buried,

neither one nor two.
As you look closer,

look like a moth
swooping, and brush

a fingertip through
this blind dazzle

tumbled out of the sky,
you can just make it out,

the miracle, a whole
drift of stars,

six-pointed, twinkling.

SOFA WELLINGTONIA

or maybe it's a bed –
the world's tallest headboard.
I install myself against
forgiving bronze corrugations
warmed by low autumn sun.

A pheasant's rusty alarm
startles me back from
sequoia dreaming,
a cushion of stilled time –
home from that sweet home

where trees are all
the furniture we need.

I want to be cleverer than I am but this is me – plain, limited. I know my place. Always in the shade. North. I've been here years, forever. Sometimes I'm tired, tired to the very ends of my hair, tired of my own patience. Part of the furniture. Cushion. Mat. All that greening and sporing is endless, invisible. Because I manage without seeds and flowers, I'm considered lower-class. Natural discrimination. Except in Japan, where they know about calm and stillness. Those temples could turn a girl's head. But here I'm allergic to brightness and have such a thirst. Unslakeable. It's one long hangover. Until all of a sudden something pops out and makes me new, softer and greener than before and it's all worthwhile. That and the small, infrequent adventures – patching soldier's wounds, putting out fires, helping make bread when times are lean. Oh yes, I can be relied on in a crisis. It's the day-to-day that wears me out

PUZZLE

Across

When the sculptor who works with wood$^{2\ \&\ 3}$claims   (5,4)
this one has nothing to say, I want to
suck the wax from his ears and feed him
a handful of seeds, piney and vibrant.

Imagine the teeth and tongue and gullet
of the dinosaurs^6 grazing the upper canopy,   (8)
the slender-billed parakeets,
the more than seventy insects that live

nowhere else. There are no monkeys in Chile
or Argentina, even if they could figure
out how to climb those spiked branches,
the prized knotless timber men have felled

Down

for railway sleepers and ladders, oars
and aeroplanes, pianos. It's sacred,
endangered, on the Red List – *pehuén*.
One Scot $^{4\ \&\ 5}$ had ears to hear when he tasted   (9,7)

its seeds served at the Governor's table
for dessert. He slipped some in his pocket
to sow on the return voyage just as
the embers of that century^1 were dying.   (10)

Five survived and their children thrive
in damp and acid soils – *Araucaria* –
beloved by those who respect whatever's hard,
beyond them, not quite black or white.

POEM WITHOUT BEES

A sound like *uzz*
flattens in a sleepy *zzz*.

Something's missing
you can't put your finger on:
lue-ell, uddleia, leeding heart.

Look at it like this:
lack and yellow.

Reakfast is toast,
unuttered,
sweetness squandered.

How soon *reath* stiffens –
wreath's rictus.

STONE MEADOW

WINTER

If your genius is the god of square things,
your fallen angel is mud, black and rutted,

just under the skin. A Pandora's box
of bones and weather, you're a sanctuary

that brings no comfort, braced against
scouring elements. You'd fold

yourself flat into a sarcophagus,
or three months' sleep at least, were it not

for the barn owl scratching his love songs
on blistered air. Always some joker

insisting on wakefulness – the nudge
of a snowdrop; hills lifted from dark

by invisible moles; one auburn hydrangea,
clinging to a limestone wall, impelled

to release itself from the terrible
thrall of your horizontals.

SPRING

Like no other garden I know, you're stubborn –
the way you resist the concept of Eden,

scramble between seasons, showers and breezes,
playing hide and seek. The passerines

sing you awake, a parabola of notes suspended
in air still with a chill in it, but clever now, gold

and blue mixed, a tincture of what's possible,
a stronger draught of shadows. You start small –

daffodils, irises, buds, all in miniature.
The lawn remains hesitant, unsure

of this endless spin about growth. I suspect you
have a secret life – at night Venus and Jupiter

and their flashy crowd make trouble
with your greenness, inchoate, susceptible:

the disappearance of the dead baby rabbit –
a case, like many others, still unsolved.

SUMMER

By the time we hit June you admit it –
velvet-petalled, honey-tongued, you're all about

sex, high as a horsefly on chlorophyll.
When I come down to your level – speedwell,

campion, buttercup – I smell danger.
Every plant for itself where the wild things grow:

the sycamore I keep trying to tame
is a tumescence of emerald; the pond a swamp,

ferns trembling beneath the weight of insects,
heavy with pollen and need. Look here,

it's inside my hips' broken sepals – desire
and nectar: what we've both been waiting for –

the longest day, that deep shiver of earth,
me giving in to your crazy whisper

forget-me-not, forget-me, forget-me-not, forget.

Autumn

Imagine Keats showing us a woman
taking off her clothes before making love

for the very last time, three sour apples
hanging on the branch above her head. You

are the room that film is set in. Unforgiving
light, tinnitus of dessicated leaves.

A few mauve wands of Michaelmas daisies
attempt some gesture of enchantment

but can't disguise your longing to be mist,
soft-focus, to segue into the certainty

of snow. You can't look me in the eye; shrug,
as if you always knew I'd lost something

I never had and there's no word for it.
How can I love you, call you home when

on the other side of the fence, they're hunting?
Hoof-beat, horn-blow, barking. I wheelbarrow

a block of stone carved with your name
beneath the windswept apple tree –

headstone and blessing, closing credits.

FLORIOGRAPHY

This is a ~~garden book~~ poem
about ~~blindness regret~~ longing.

All that's left of it
are ~~letters~~ ghosts ~~petals~~.

Bury it in the ~~bed soil~~ dark
where no flowers grow.

History will ~~blacken rewrite~~
transplant the lines:

sickles / seeds / grenades
marigold / honesty / pomegranate.

Never ~~again, never~~ again.

TEA SUTRA

Just-boiled water shocks it
    into life, this pygmy head
    striped with grey, like my own;
the cage of leaves unlocked
        sets petals
loose,
       a carnival of orange tongues,
creased from tight silence,
             a roaring now
of coral and vein, feline –
          until
    out springs   a long song   of blossom,
a white glory   of an utterance. So
I wait while it brews,
    till it's cool enough to drink;
let the catechins, kaempferol, quercetin
        and caffeine,
    all the wild things,
spike this tongue of mine,
    coax out the flowers
       hiding inside my mouth.

HAW MEDICINE

Crataegus monogyna

Because there are days
and, more often, nights
when words aren't enough
and the ones we find
uncurling from our minds
or lips fail to take root,
I want to plant you
a hedge of hawthorn.
Named from *kratos*, strength,
it brings the singular gift
of pitching the hardest
grain against the softest
petal. I offer you this.
Settle back and rest,
watch the black stems
spring into bud, leaf; a film
that captures time, *tick*,
tick, then releases it.
Let the precious blossom,
clusters of sex and death,
waft their hag-blessed musk
and take you as they will;
a spell to blow the dust
off your winter skin,
what's buried under it,
shy of the lifting light.
May the riddle of thorn
keep you from harm,
remind you of home,
someone, somewhere
whose job it is to take you
in; those open arms,

strong enough to bear
whatever fruit tastes good
to birds, and us,
waxwing and thrush.

BIRD'S-EYE

When the world's spinning too fast
and I feel as if I might wing off
at any moment, I take that moment

to say *green alkanet*, seeding the air
with its four disparate syllables.
Flowers of sky-fallen blue balance

on stubbly stems, pricked with flocking
birds' eyes that blink at cow parsley
wedded on a summer roadside.

Virgilian, in exile from myself,
I sing *Pentaglottis sempervirens*;
may I too be five-tongued, everlasting,

honour my neighbours— field scabious,
fresh honesty – weigh the difference
between what should be fenced off,

what tugged out or mown down.
While a May wind's insisting on speed
and blur, today this cool blueness

is enough to hold me still, stay
where I need to be – the ballast
of its green name, red roots,

the long, unceasing moment.

KNITBONE

Symphytum officinale

Don't be fooled by my soft folds,
I feed earth and fix bones.
My tuberous roots, hidden
as all the best things are,
    mend what is broken:
    the cue of all my names
for curing, soothing what is sore.
Unsundering. If you know
    what you need, why ignore
    the remedy? Let me bring my way
with bones to all your blindness.
Look again at my pleated creams:
    See how I am bell and lantern.
    Breathe in this smell of morning rain.

LINDISFARNE SILVERWEED

Argentina anserina

You send me a pilgrim-monk's-eye view –
our lord's footsteps, cinquefoil – gold and silver
sprung out of the sand, foliage like feathers, spray.
Crimson runners are lines on a manuscript,
join what needs to be joined, arteries

of earth and heart: the shudder of the sea
not far away; a sadness in the stretch
and snap of the waves, the way they suck themselves
back, sadder. You steer your course with such grace,
a brother's footsteps I try to follow

and ask for nothing – amazed when what blooms
in the imprint of each carefully planted heel
and toe is a sudden illumination
of silver and gold. A chance for the mutual,
that amniotic salt we've been berthed in,

over and over. All I need to do
is open the book of my heart and keep on
looking. Here, traveller – *goosewort, richette* –
tuck some fresh leaves inside your shoes
to leaven the crossing, our long walking.

RYOAN-JI

Not a collector of light, a breaker
of dark, all I can bring you home
are fifteen rocks to watch yourself by;

the *oku* stone, heart and soul,
forever elusive. Still, I blow you less
than an ounce of warm breath,

that spark when two rocks are struck
together. Now you see it, now its ghost –
how much light a stone can hold.

NA TROSAICHEAN

Away in the glen, loch on one side,
mountain on the other, someone's planted
a garden. It takes more than simple hope
to barrow ten tons of gravel and spade
and rake it level round the L-shaped beds,
to coax those plants into flower strong enough
to dance with the season's short span –
tangled nasturtiums, astrantia's tethered stars.

It's a gesture towards what's possible,
our instinct for cultivation, how much care
we can bring to the wild landscapes unmapped
inside us. Bull's-eye, a hedge of box
shelters four pear trees trained in a spiral
towards open sky and the promise of harvest.

PARACHUTISTS

After Guiseppe Bartolini's lithograph, Pisa

Jellyfish fall through the heavens above
the viridescent night of the Orto Botanico.

Count their drifting moons, skullcaps
for the duomo, just visible over the wall – 7, 8,

9. In fact, they're all parachutists: cumulative grace
at odds with their singular mission; that history

still untold. Let's say today they wear the ruched silk
of angels, landing within the garden's jurisdiction.

Watch them unhook their spent umbrellas and pick up
a spade to dig fresh beds or a rake to sweep paths

clear. They'll unravel the hose to revive parched myrtle
or pelargoniums; reinstate tumbled ceramic, fix

cracked signs and screw the last bolt in new glasshouses.
As the city sleeps, they'll delve till the trees toll

their boughs in exaltation, each one seen so hard
the people will wake up to the world's first day.

THE YEAR THE FIELDS SHONE

Too easily overlooked,
this gold beneath our feet:

your name so quick on our tongue
zips our eyes shut.

If we called you *sitfast*
or *little frog* instead

would we find the flower
within the flower,

remember what's forgotten –
a love of butter,

our own throat's radiance?

and you are there and the garden is there.
As near to kin as you'll ever be,
close-cut lawn billowing all about you,
your eyes turn countless shades of green.
Hidden like a pip inside an apple,
you hold the keys to Eden. Here you are free,
not wishing the world were otherwise
nor wanting one whit to change.
　　　　Its flag is change,
this small republic of manna ash
and buckeye, mandrake and gunnera,
sparrowsong trickling through the air like hope.
A garden's properly owned by no one:
doesn't it belong to us all? Who's to say
on which side of the gate the dream begins?

On which side of the gate does the dream begin?
Who's to say? Doesn't it all belong to us?
Like a garden, properly owned by no one?
Sparrowsong trickles through the air like hope,
through buckeye and mandrake and gunnera.
In this small republic of manna ash
　　　　our flag is change –
so why ask change to change
or wish the world were otherwise?
You hold the keys to Eden: here you are free,
hidden like a pip inside an apple.
Your eyes turn countless shades of green,
close-cut lawn billowing all about you.
As near to kin as you'll ever be.
And you are there and the garden is there.

LINDA FRANCE lives close to Hadrian's Wall, near Hexham in Northumberland. Since 1992, she has published eight poetry collections with Bloodaxe, Smokestack and Arc, including *The Gentleness of the Very Tall* (a Poetry Book Society Recommendation), *The Toast of the Kit-Cat Club*, *book of days* (a 'year renga') and *You are Her*. *Reading the Flowers* began during a Leverhulme Residency at Moorbank, Newcastle University's Botanic Garden, in 2010-11, which led to a 'grand tour' of thirteen Botanic Gardens in the UK and abroad.

Linda has worked on a number of collaborations with visual artists, particularly in the realm of Public Art. She also edited the ground-breaking anthology *Sixty Women Poets* (Bloodaxe 1993, a Poetry Book Society Special Commendation). Linda was awarded the Arts Foundation's first Poetry Fellowship. She won First Prize in the 2013 National Poetry Competition and is currently Creative Writing Fellow at the University of Leeds.

Selected titles in Arc Publications'
POETRY FROM THE UK / IRELAND include:

D. M. BLACK
Claiming Kindred

JAMES BYRNE
Blood / Sugar
White Coins

DONALD ATKINSON
In Waterlight:
Poems New, Selected & Revised

JOANNA BOULTER
Twenty Four Preludes & Fugues on
Dmitri Shostakovich

TONY CURTIS
What Darkness Covers
The Well in the Rain
folk
Approximately in the Key of C

JULIA DARLING
Indelible, Miraculous
COLLECTED POEMS

LINDA FRANCE
You are Her

KATHERINE GALLAGHER
Circus-Apprentice
Carnival Edge

CHRISSIE GITTINS
Armature

RICHARD GWYN
Sad Giraffe Café

GLYN HUGHES
A Year in the Bull-Box

MICHAEL HASLAM
The Music Laid Her Songs in Language
A Sinner Saved by Grace
A Cure for Woodness

MICHAEL HULSE
The Secret History
Half-Life

CHRISTOPHER JAMES
Farewell to the Earth

BRIAN JOHNSTONE
The Book of Belongings
Dry Stone Work

JOEL LANE
Trouble in the Heartland
The Autumn Myth

HERBERT LOMAS
The Vale of Todmorden
A Casual Knack of Living
COLLECTED POEMS

SOPHIE MAYER
(O)

PETE MORGAN
August Light

MICHAEL O'NEILL
Wheel
Gangs of Shadow

MARY O'DONNELL
The Ark Builders
Those April Fevers

IAN POPLE
An Occasional Lean-to
Saving Spaces

PAUL STUBBS
The Icon Maker
The End of the Trial of Man

LORNA THORPE
A Ghost in My House
Sweet Torture of Breathing

ROISIN TIERNEY
The Spanish-Italian Border

MICHELENE WANDOR
Musica Transalpina
Music of the Prophets
Natural Chemistry

JACKIE WILLS
Fever Tree
Commandments
Woman's Head as Jug